UNDER THE
microscope

FUNGI
IN OUR WORLD

WRITTEN BY JOHN WOOD

> I'M FREDDIE THE
> FUNGUS, AND THIS IS MY
> FRIEND, MILLIE MUSHROOM.
> WE'LL BE YOUR GUIDES IN
> YOUR JOURNEY UNDER
> THE MICROSCOPE!

Millie

Freddie

KidHaven
PUBLISHING

Published in 2020 by
**KidHaven Publishing, an Imprint of
Greenhaven Publishing, LLC**
353 3rd Avenue
Suite 255
New York, NY 10010

Edited by: Kirsty Holmes
Designed by: Amy Li

Cataloging-in-Publication Data

Names: Wood, John.
Title: Fungi in our world / John Wood.
Description: New York : KidHaven Publishing, 2020. | Series: Under the microscope | Includes glossary and index.
Identifiers: ISBN 9781534533172 (pbk.) | ISBN 9781534533196 (library bound) | ISBN 9781534533189 (6 pack) | ISBN 9781534533202 (ebook)
Subjects: LCSH: Fungi--Juvenile literature. | Molds (Fungi)--Juvenile literature.
Classification: LCC QK603.5 W663 2020 | DDC 579.5--dc23

Printed in the United States of America

CPSIA compliance information: Batch #BW20KL: For further information contact Greenhaven Publishing LLC, New York, New York at 1-844-317-7404.

Please visit our website, www.greenhavenpublishing.com. For a free color catalog of all our high-quality books, call toll free 1-844-317-7404 or fax 1-844-317-7405.

CONTENTS

WORDS THAT LOOK LIKE THIS CAN BE FOUND IN THE GLOSSARY ON PAGE 24.

WHAT ARE FUNGI?

Fungi are living things that are different from plants and animals. Fungi come in all sorts of shapes, sizes, and colors.

SCARLET ELF CUP FUNGUS

MOLD IS ALSO A TYPE OF FUNGUS.

Fungi break down things in nature, such as old plants, food, and dead animals. This is what is happening when mold grows on food. The mold is breaking down the food.

WHAT IS A MICROSCOPE?

Microscopes are used to see very small things that can't be seen with just our eyes. There is a whole world of living things that would be **invisible** to us without a microscope.

MICROSCOPE

Some microscopes are more powerful than others. Scientists use very powerful microscopes, like the one in the picture below.

MUSHROOMS

You might have seen mushrooms growing on the ground. However, under the ground there might be a whole **network** of fungi connecting many mushrooms together.

MUSHROOM

MYCELIUM

THE NETWORK IS CALLED THE MYCELIUM (SAY: MY-SEE-LEE-UM). IT IS LIKE THE ROOTS OF THE MUSHROOM.

The part of the mushroom you can see is called the fruiting body. The fruiting body creates spores. Spores are like seeds – they spread out and grow into new fungi.

SOME OUTDOOR MUSHROOMS GROW IN A CIRCLE.

LET'S TURN THE PAGE AND LOOK UNDER THE MICROSCOPE!

Spores can only grow into fungi if they have the things that they need. They need a place that is wet and warm, with plenty of **nutrients** around.

THIS AREA, UNDER THE HEAD OF THE MUSHROOM, IS CALLED THE GILLS. SPORES CAN COME FROM HERE.

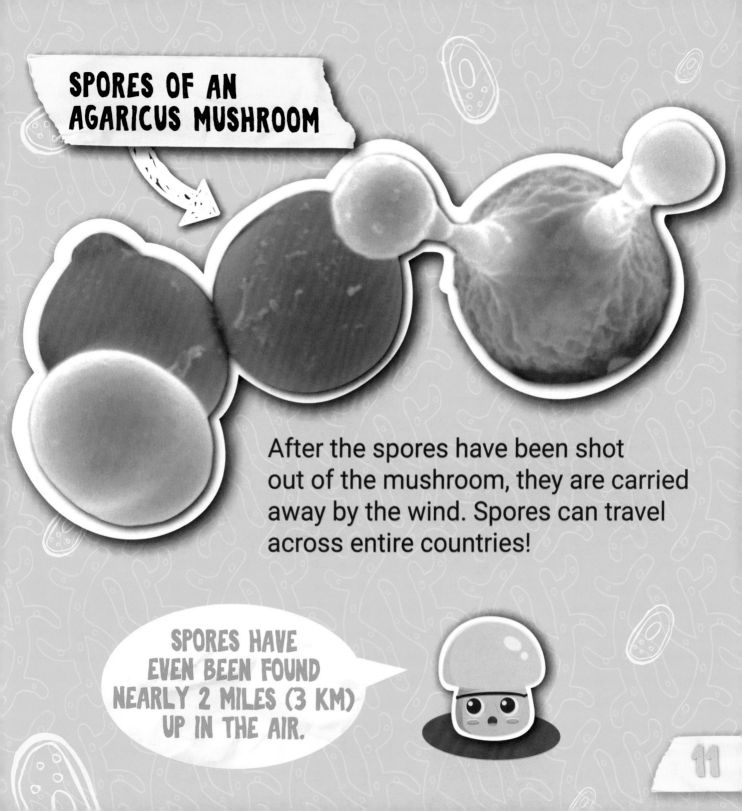

SPORES OF AN AGARICUS MUSHROOM

After the spores have been shot out of the mushroom, they are carried away by the wind. Spores can travel across entire countries!

SPORES HAVE EVEN BEEN FOUND NEARLY 2 MILES (3 KM) UP IN THE AIR.

SHELF FUNGI

Shelf fungi are often found in the woods, where they grow on trees. They are actually eating the trees, and can weaken or even break the trees down.

SOME TYPES OF SHELF FUNGUS CAN RELEASE AROUND 5 TRILLION SPORES EVERY YEAR.

Whether it is mold or mushrooms, all fungi eat in the same way. Fungi get nutrients by eating away at natural things.

THE UNDERSIDE OF A SHELF FUNGUS

LET'S TURN THE PAGE AND LOOK UNDER THE MICROSCOPE!

All fungi are made up of tiny hyphae (say: hi-fee), which are a bit like small **fibers**. Sometimes the hyphae join up to make a fuzzy cloud, like mold. Sometimes they make a spongy object, like a mushroom cap.

THESE ARE THE HYPHAE THAT MAKE UP A MUSHROOM.

Fungi eat by oozing enzymes. Enzymes are chemicals that break things down. There are enzymes in your stomach and your spit that help to break down food.

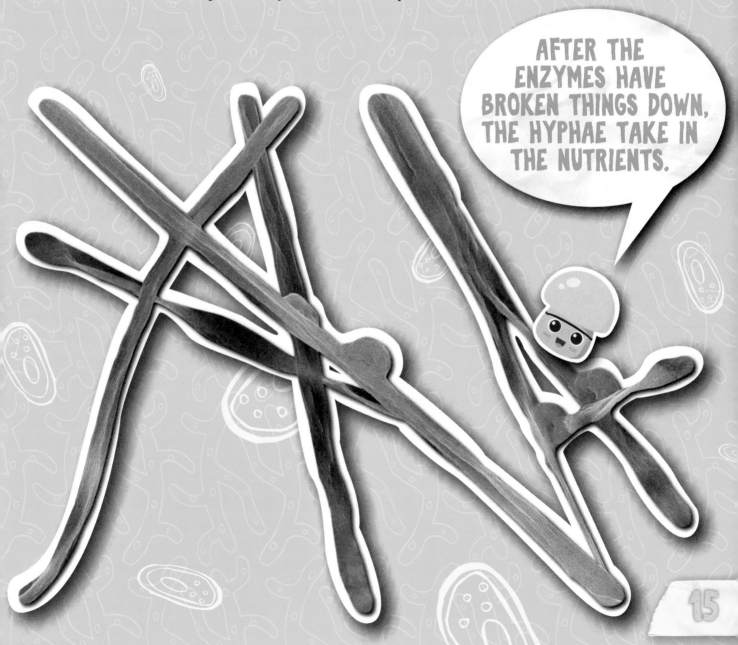

AFTER THE ENZYMES HAVE BROKEN THINGS DOWN, THE HYPHAE TAKE IN THE NUTRIENTS.

MOLD

Fungi and bacteria cause old food, dead plants, and dead animals to rot away. The nutrients that make up these natural things can then be used again. But mold can be useful in other ways, too.

Mold is used to make some types of cheese. There are also types of mold that kill harmful bacteria. For example, penicillin comes from a mold called *Penicillium* and is used to create medicine such as antibiotics.

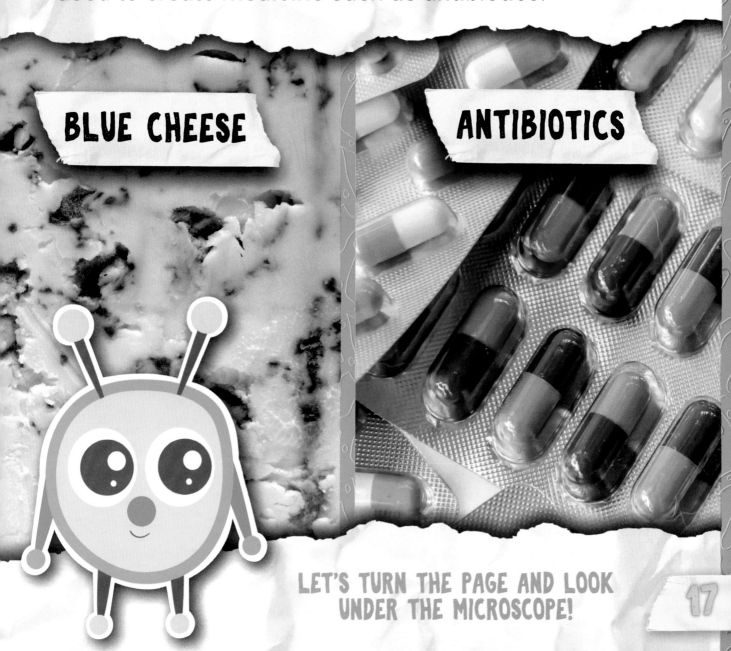

BLUE CHEESE

ANTIBIOTICS

LET'S TURN THE PAGE AND LOOK
UNDER THE MICROSCOPE!

17

Penicillin was discovered by accident. When a scientist named Alexander Fleming came back from vacation, he noticed mold growing on a dish that had been left out. This type of mold had killed all the bacteria around it.

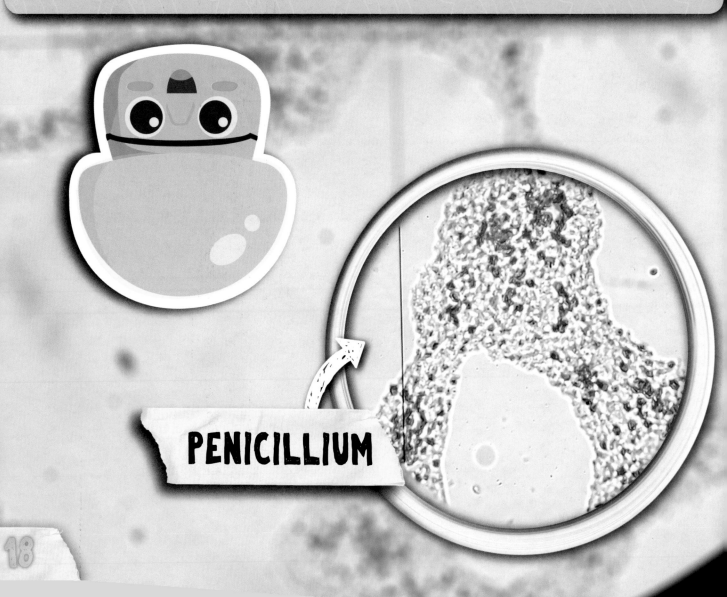

PENICILLIUM

Some mold is harmful to humans.
If someone breathed in lots and lots
of mold spores, they could get very ill.

YEAST

Yeast is a very small type of fungus, and is found all over the world. Humans have found lots of uses for yeast.

YEAST IS USED TO MAKE BREAD.

Yeast makes bread dough rise before it goes in the oven. This is because yeast releases gas, which inflates the dough like a balloon.

BREAD DOUGH

LET'S TURN THE PAGE AND LOOK UNDER THE MICROSCOPE!

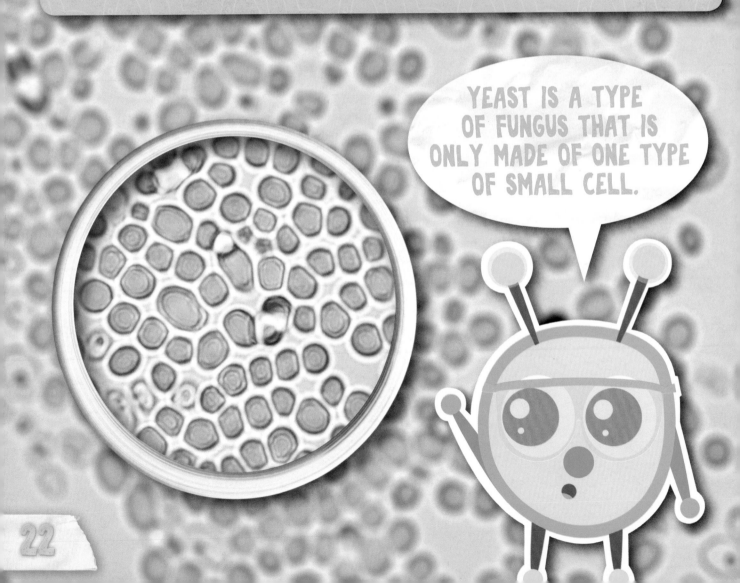

All living things are made up of cells. Cells are like tiny building blocks. Animals, plants, and lots of fungi are made up of millions, billions, or even trillions of different cells, all joined together.

New yeast cells grow on the side of old ones – these new cells are called buds. Buds break off when they are big enough.

MOST YEAST CELLS ARE AROUND 0.004 MILLIMETER WIDE.

NOW YOU KNOW ALL ABOUT THE TINY, INVISIBLE WORLD OF FUNGI. WHAT OTHER THINGS WOULD YOU LIKE TO SEE UNDER THE MICROSCOPE?

GLOSSARY

BACTERIA   microscopic living things that can cause diseases

CHEMICALS   substances that materials are made from

FIBERS   things that are like threads

GAS   an air-like substance that expands freely to fill any space available

INVISIBLE   cannot be seen

MOLD   a type of fungus that rots away natural things that are old or dead

NETWORK   a system of connected people or things

NUTRIENTS   natural substances that plants and animals need to grow and stay healthy

SCIENTISTS   people who study and know a lot about science

TRILLION   the number 1,000,000,000,000, which is equal to 1,000 billion

INDEX